piano • vocal • guitar

JAMES BROWN
The Ultimate Collection

TABLE OF CONTENTS

ISBN 978-1-4768-8938-2

HAL•LEONARD®
CORPORATION

7777 W. Bluemound Rd. P.O. Box 13819 Milwaukee, WI 53213

In Australia Contact:
Hal Leonard Australia Pty. Ltd.
4 Lentara Court
Cheltenham, Victoria, 3192 Australia
Email: ausadmin@halleonard.com.au

Visit Hal Leonard Online at
www.halleonard.com

COLD SWEAT, PT. 1

Words and Music by JAMES BROWN
and ALFRED JAMES ELLIS

I don't care a - bout your past, ___ I just
I don't care a - bout your won'ts, ___ I just

want ___ our love to last. ___ I don't care
wan-na tell you ___ 'bout your do's ___ and don'ts. I don't care

a - bout your faults, I just want ___
a - bout the way you treat me, dar - ling, I just want ___

to sat - is - fy your thoughts. ⌐
to un - der - stand me al - ways. ⌐

When you kiss me, _____ when you miss me,

hold __ my hand, _____ make me un - der - stand. __

D.C.
D.C. and Fade

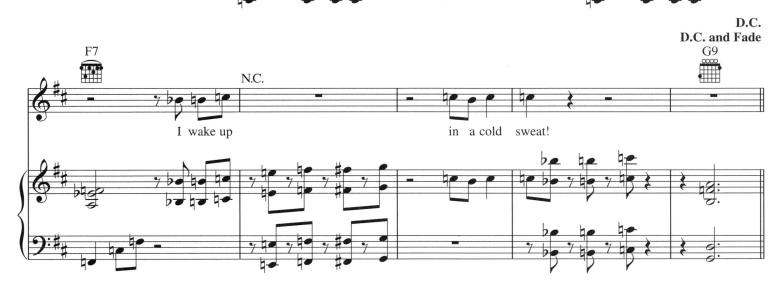

I wake up in a cold sweat!

DOIN' IT TO DEATH

Words and Music by
JAMES BROWN

funk good time. We got - ta take you high -

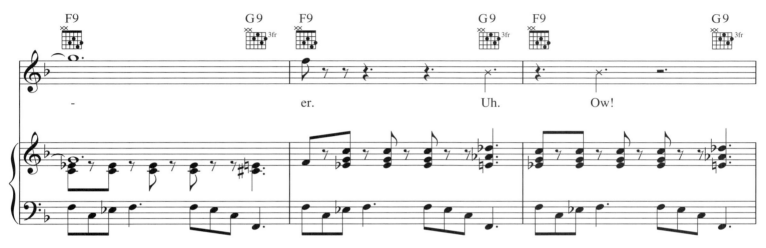

- er. Uh. Ow!

We gonna do it again.

I got - ta take you

Brothers? Now I want everybody, let's play and blow about two choruses,

Play 3 times

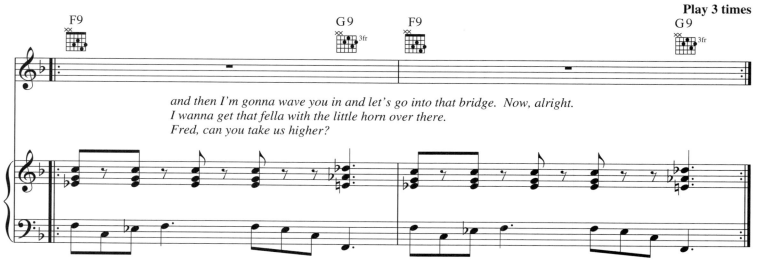

and then I'm gonna wave you in and let's go into that bridge. Now, alright.
I wanna get that fella with the little horn over there.
Fred, can you take us higher?

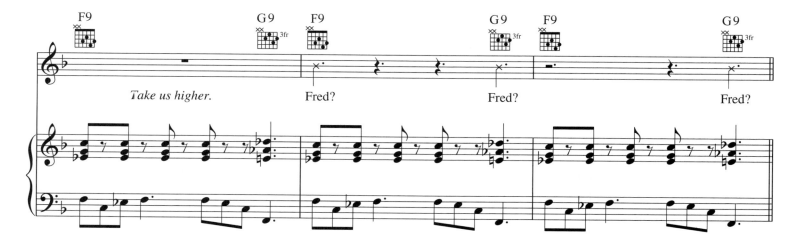

Take us higher.   *Fred?*   *Fred?*   *Fred?*

Repeat as needed

Instrumental solo

You know what? When I hear a groove like this groove...   Oh,

I say, I got to take it high

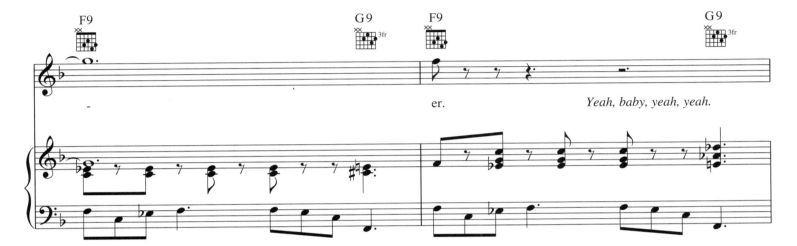

- er. *Yeah, baby, yeah, yeah.*

Vocal ad lib.

Repeat as needed

Last time

We got-ta have a

Play 4 times

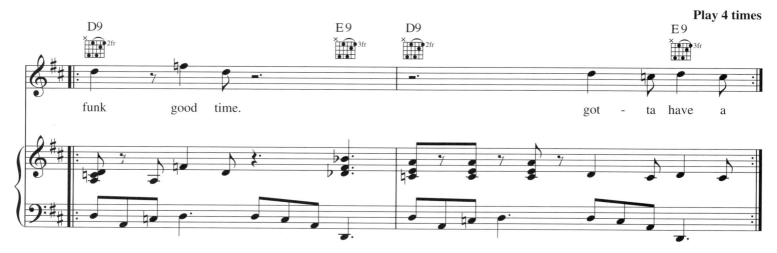

funk good time. got - ta have a

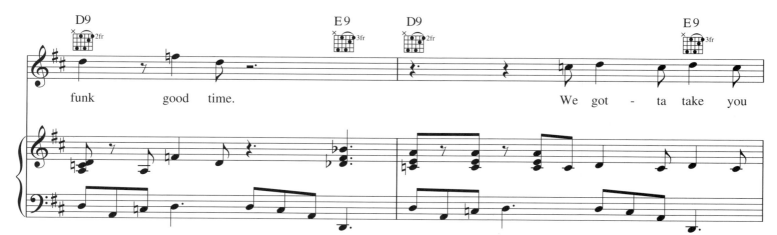

funk good time. We got - ta take you

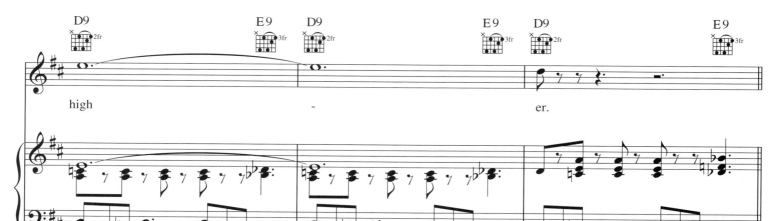

high - er.

Repeat and Fade

Optional Ending

Vocal ad lib. to end

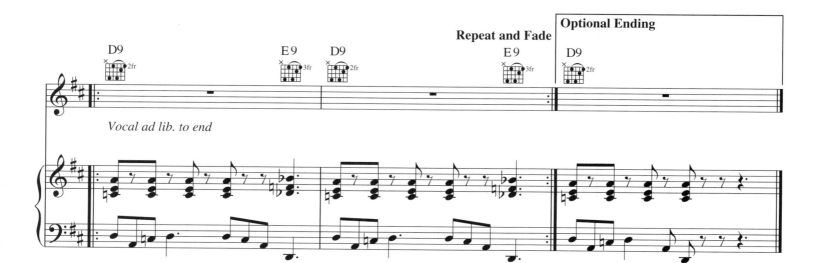

GET ON THE GOOD FOOT

Words and Music by JAMES BROWN,
FRED WESLEY and JOE MIMS

Funky

Shouted: Que pasa, people, que pasa?

Get on down

I wan-na get on the good foot   good foot   I got to

get on the good foot - a   Go-in' down to the crib   and let it all hang

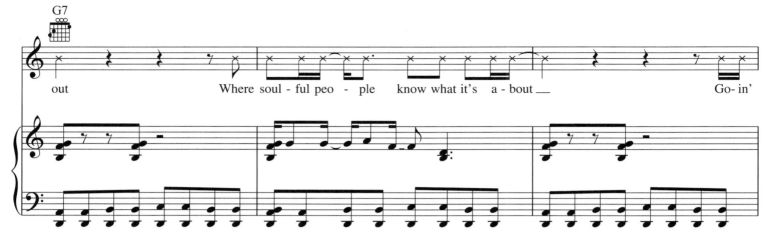

out Where soul-ful peo - ple know what it's a - bout __ Go-in'

down to the crib and let it all hang out Where soul-ful peo - ple know what it's a - bout __

__ Where peo-ple give a sign and take __ your hand __ And

dance un - til the mu - sic of the day - time band __ They're danc - in' on the

Additional Lyrics

I say the long-haired hippies and the Afro basket
All together when the clock strikes
And they party on the good foot
You know they' dancin' on the good foot
Ain't nothin' goin' on but the rhythm
A whole lotta bills and m' money spent
And that's on m' bad foot
You know m' pay is gettin' short, I've got the blues
I got a funky job and I pay m' dues
On the good foot. (etc.)

GET UP
(I Feel Like Being)
A SEX MACHINE

Words and Music by JAMES BROWN,
BOBBY BYRD and RONALD LENHOFF

Shout: Fellas, I'm ready to get up and do my thing.
I wanta get into it, man, you know...
Like a, like a sex machine, man,
Movin'... doin' it, you know
Can I count it off? (Go ahead)

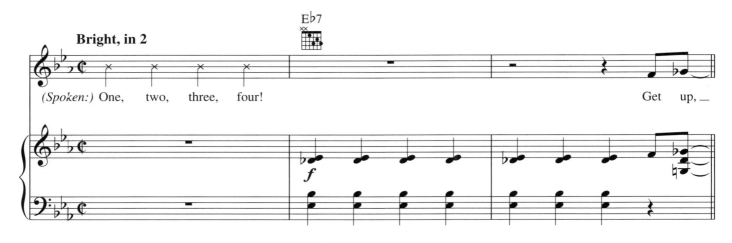

(Spoken:) One, two, three, four!

Get up, ___

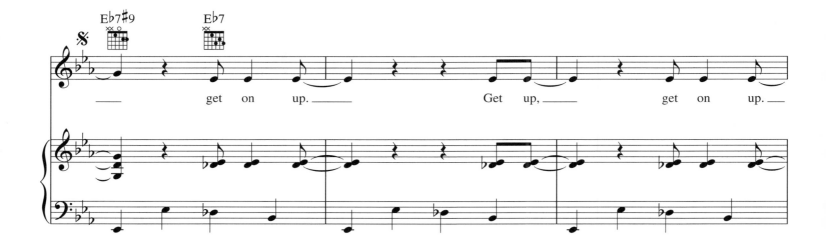

___ get on up. ___ Get up, ___ get on up.

___ Stay on the scene, get on up, ___ like a sex ma- chine. ___

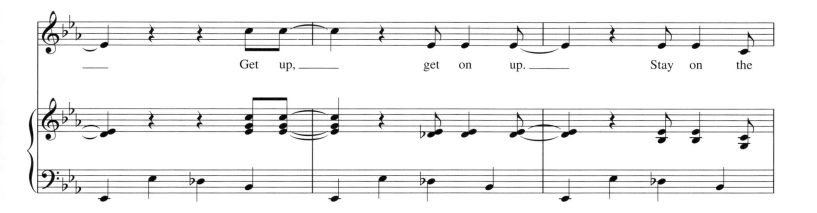

scene, get on up, ___ like a sex ma - chine. ___ Get on up. ___

Eb7#9   Eb7

___ Wait a min - ute!   1. Shake your ___ arm   then
                          2. *(See additional lyrics)*

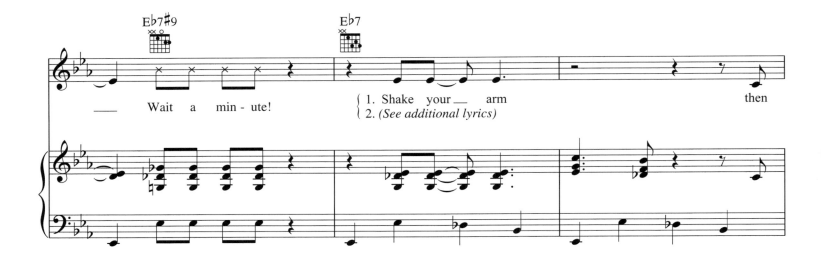

use your form. ___   Stay on the scene

Cm/Eb

like a sex ma - chine. ___   You

got to have the feel - ing

E♭m7

sure as you're born. ___

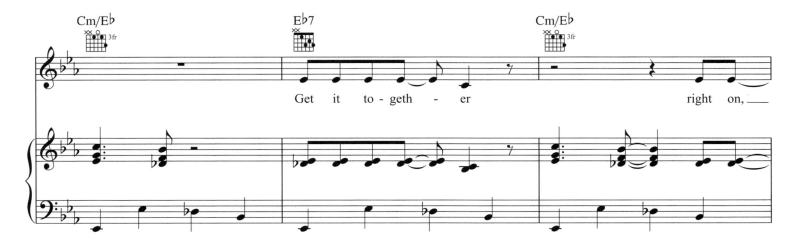

Cm/E♭

Get it to - geth - er

E♭7

Cm/E♭

right on, ___

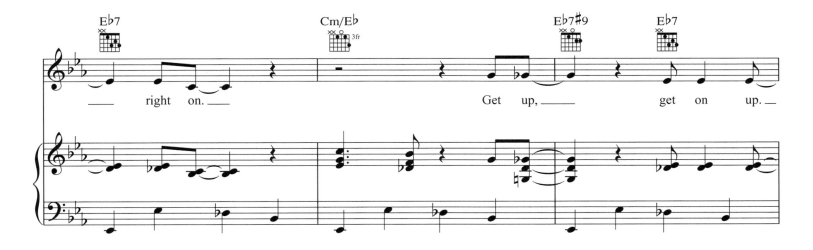

E♭7

___ right on. ___

Cm/E♭

E♭7♯9   E♭7

Get up, ___   get on up. ___

Get up, ___   get on up. ___   Get up, ___

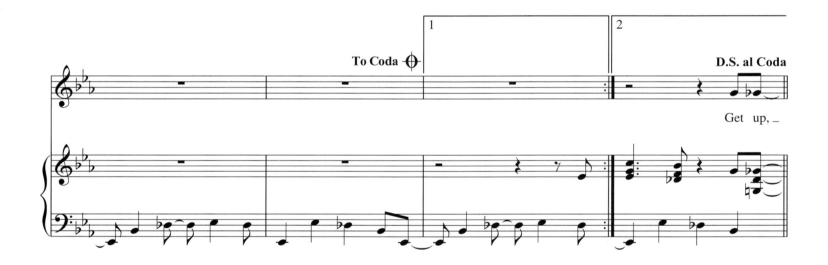

Additional Lyrics

2. I said the feeling you got to get,
   Give me the fever in a cold sweat.
   The way I like it is the way it is;
   I got mine and don't worry 'bout his.

   Get on up and then shake your money maker,
   Shake your money maker, etc.

GET UP OFFA THAT THING

Words and Music by DEANNA BROWN,
DEIDRA BROWN and YAMMA BROWN

Get up off - a that thing and dance and you'll sing it, ___ now.
Get up off - a that thing and shake it, sing it, ___ now.
Get up off - a that thing and shake it, sing it, ___ now.

Get up off - a that thing and dance and you'll _ feel bet - ter.
Get up off - a that thing and shake it, you'll _ feel bet - ter.
Get up off - a that thing and twist it, you'll _ feel bet - ter.

1

Get up off - a that thing and try to re - lease that pres - sure.
Get up off - a that thing and
Get up off - a that thing and

2, 3

F9

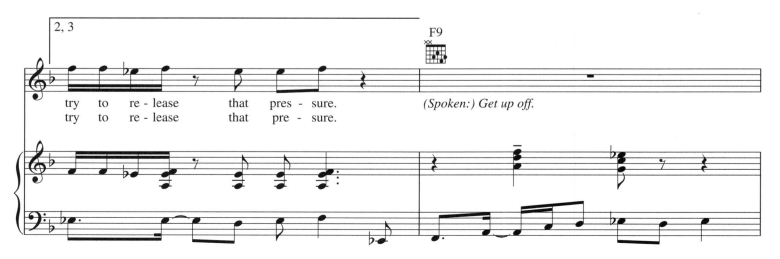

try to re - lease that pres - sure. *(Spoken:) Get up off.*
try to re - lease that pres - sure.

Good God. *So good.*

To Coda ⊕

Everybody ready?

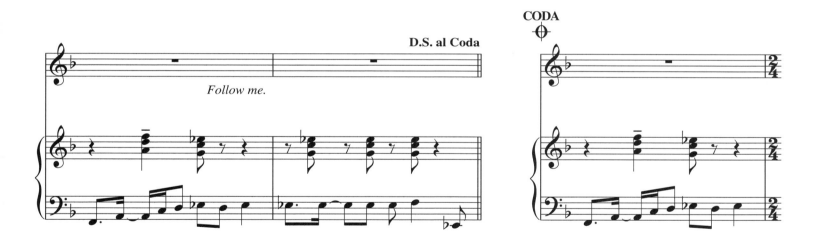

D.S. al Coda

CODA ⊕

Follow me.

Cm7   F7#9

Repeat and Fade

GIVE IT UP OR TURNIT A LOOSE

Words and Music by
CHARLES BOBBITT

Slowly, with a double-time feeling

by, give it up, turn it loose. ___

Ba - by, give it up, turn it loose. ___

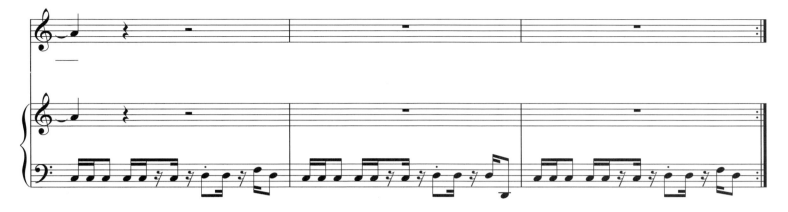

Ba - by, give it up, turn it loose. __

Hold - ing on, __
Hold ya tight, __

al - right, _____　　　　　　　　　　　hold - ing
with　　all　my　might, _　　　　　　　hold ya

on __　　　　　ain't no　　use. _
tight _　　　　'cause I　　love ya so. __

2nd time D.C. and Fade

I GOT THE FEELIN'

Words and Music by
JAMES BROWN

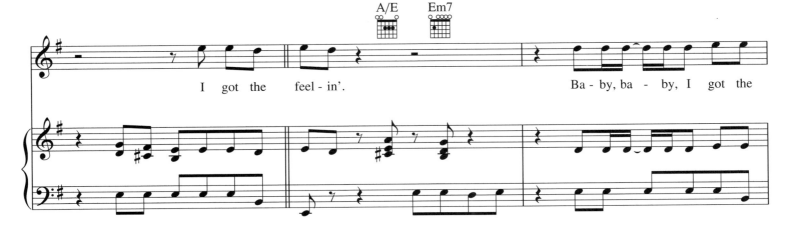

I got the feel-in'. Ba-by, ba-by, I got the

feel-in'. You don't know

what you do to me. Peo-ple are

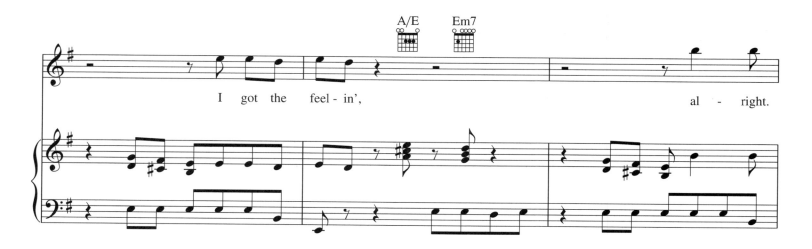

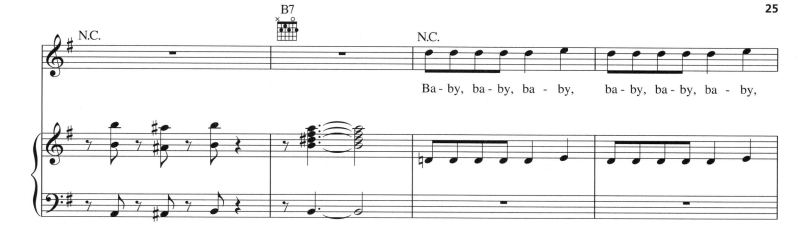

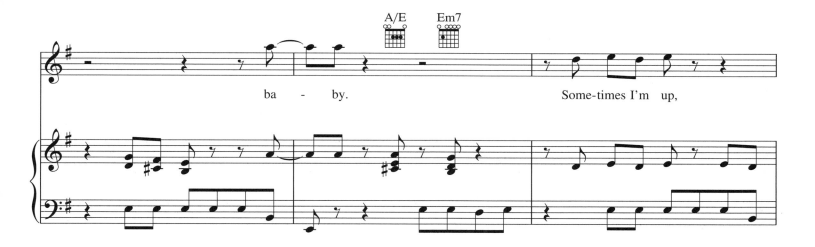

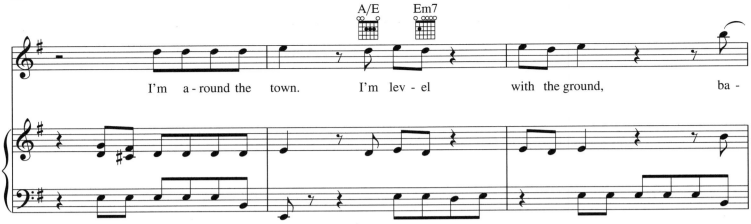

I'm a - round the town. I'm lev - el with the ground, ba -

- by, I say lev - el with the ground,

oh. _____

No, I know, no, you don't

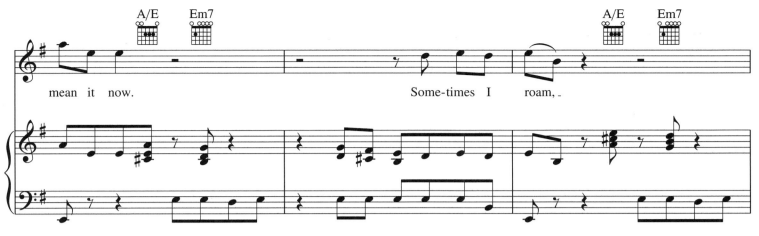

mean it now.   Some-times I roam, ___

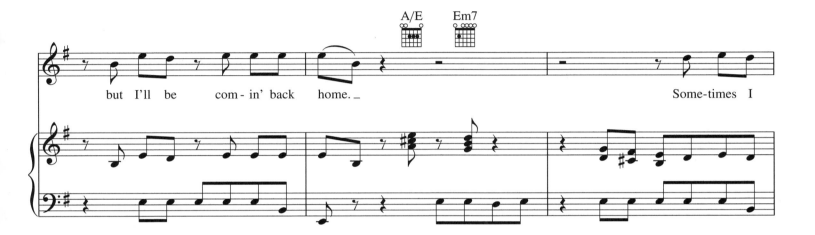

but I'll be com - in' back home. ___   Some-times I

seem to be fly; ___   I just don't know when to say bye - bye,

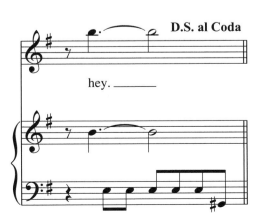

D.S. al Coda

hey. ___

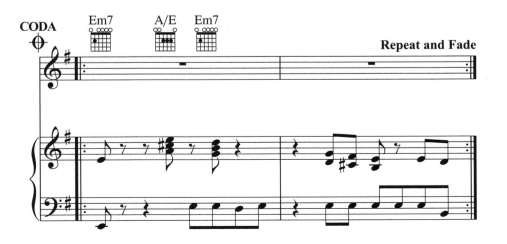

CODA

Repeat and Fade

GOOD GOOD LOVIN'

Words and Music by JAMES BROWN
and ALBERT SHUBERT

* Optional notes indicate recorded drum fills.

Good lov - in', ___ good lov - in' made me feel so nev - er thought it was

glad. _____
you. _____

Got some-thin' for you, Ow!

True, fine lov - in', a whole lot - ta hug - gin'.

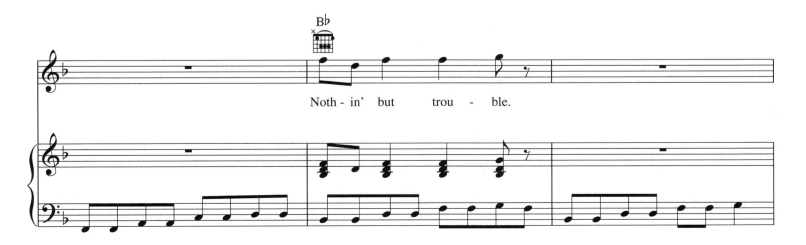

Noth - in' but trou - ble.

Ba - by, I need _____ your good lov - in'. Got some - thin' for you,

dar - lin', that you nev - er nev - er had. _____

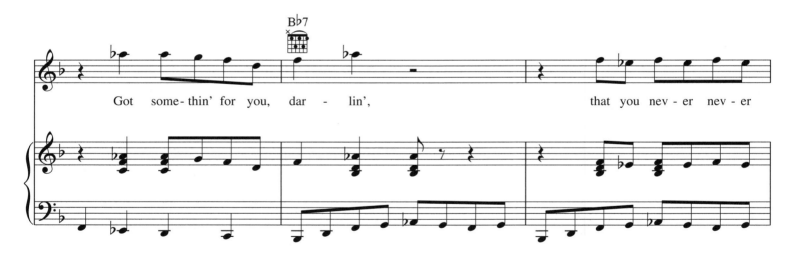

Got some - thin' for you, dar - lin', that you nev - er nev - er

had. _____ Good lov - in', ___

good lov - in' made me feel so glad. _____

Sax solo

True, fine lov - in', a

whole lot - ta hug - gin'. Noth - in' but trou - ble.

Ba - by, I need _____ your good lov - in'.

I GOT YOU
(I Feel Good)

Words and Music by
JAMES BROWN

I knew that I would ___ now.
Ah, sug - ar and spice. _____

So good,
So nice,

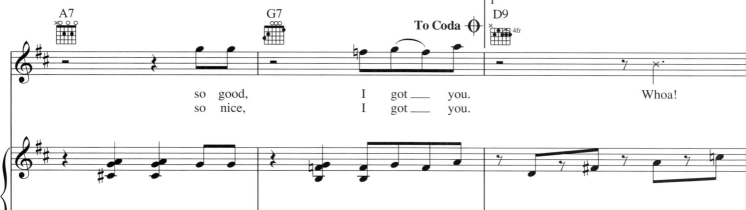

so good,
so nice,

I got ___ you.
I got ___ you.

Whoa!

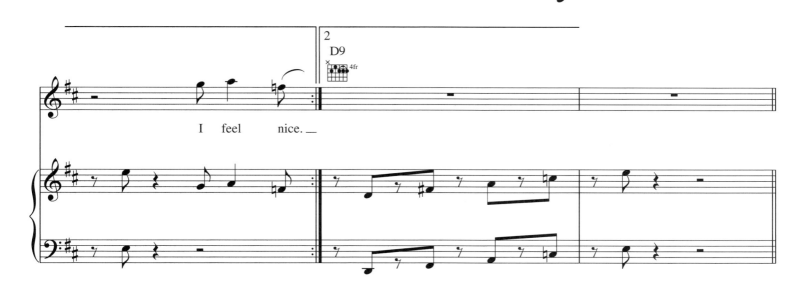

I feel nice. ___

I feel _____ nice.

Ah, sug - ar and spice. _____ So nice,

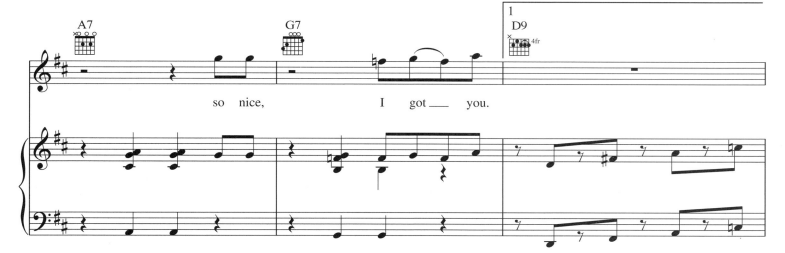

so nice, I got ___ you.

D.S. al Coda
(take 1st lyric)

Whoa! I feel good. _

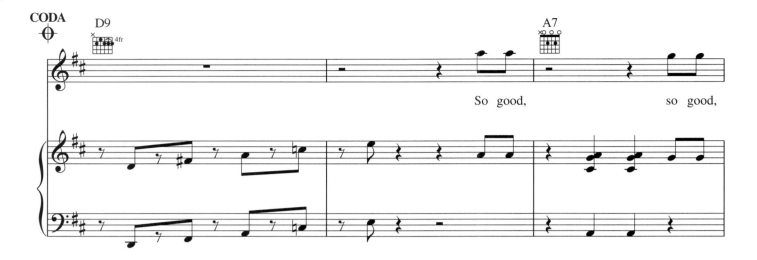

So good, so good,

'cause I got ___ you. So good,

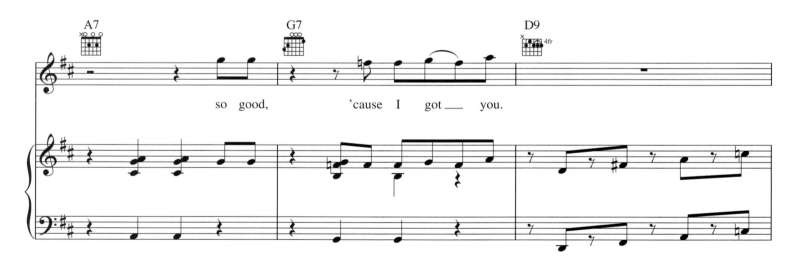

so good, 'cause I got ___ you.

Hey!

rit.

I'LL GO CRAZY

Words and Music by
JAMES BROWN

much. _____ If you quit _ You _ got to

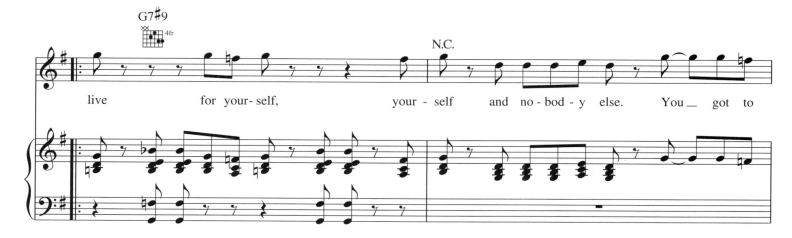

live for your- self, your - self and no-bod - y else. You _ got to

live for your- self, your - self and no-bod - y else. If you leave _

_ me, _____ I'll _____ go cra - zy. _ If you leave _ me, _____ I'll _____

go cra - zy. ___ 'Cause I love you, love you, oh, ___

___ love you too ___ much. ___ You ___ got to

love you, love you, oh, ___ I love you too much. ___

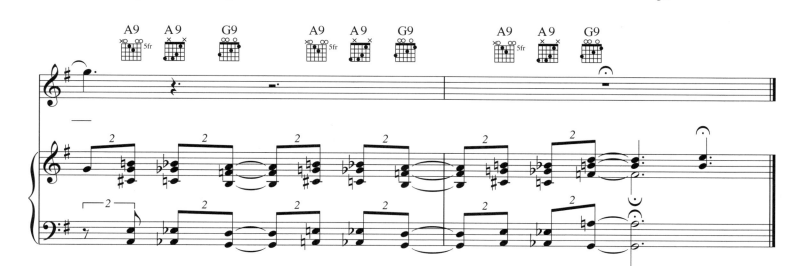

IT'S A MAN'S MAN'S MAN'S WORLD

Words and Music by JAMES BROWN
and BETTY NEWSOME

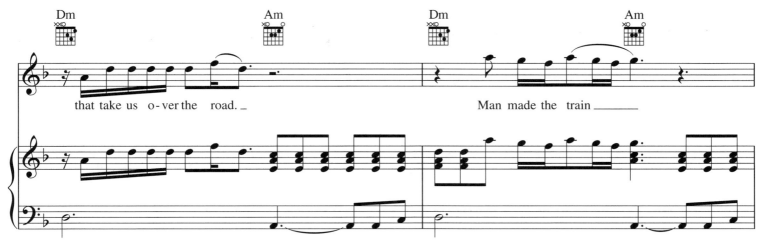

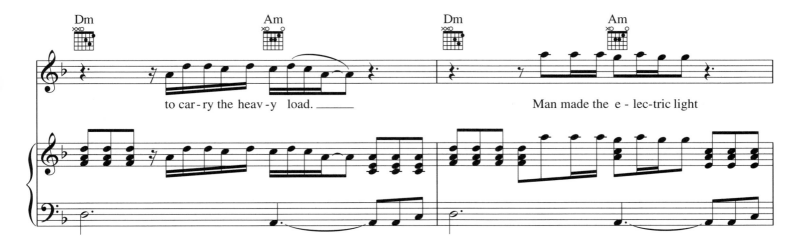

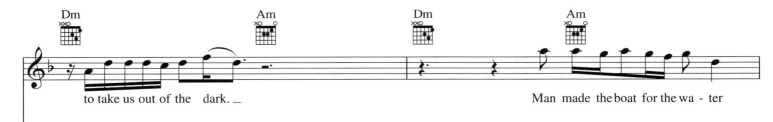

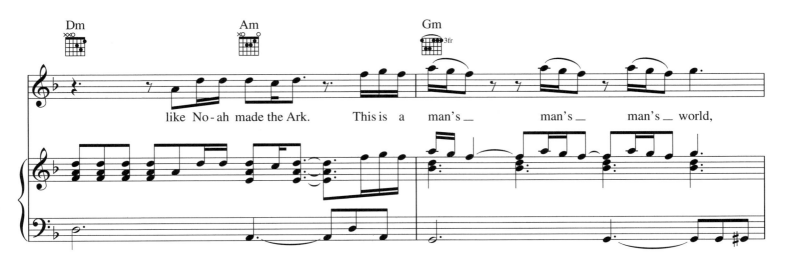

Additional Lyrics

Man thinks about the little bitty baby girls and the baby boys.
Man makes them happy 'cause man makes them toys.
And after man makes everything, everything he can
You know that man makes money to buy from other men.
This is a man's world, but it wouldn't be nothing
Without a woman or a girl.

PAPA DON'T TAKE NO MESS

Words and Music by JAMES BROWN,
FRED WESLEY, CHARLES BOBBITT
and JOHN STARKS

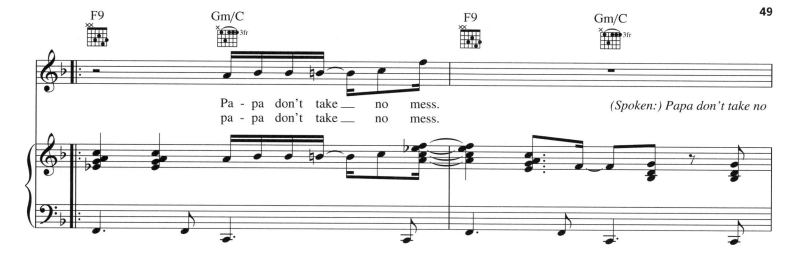

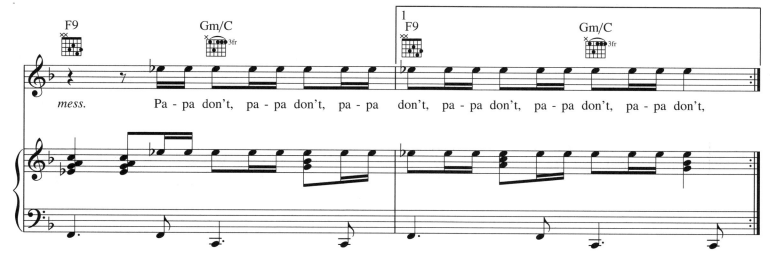

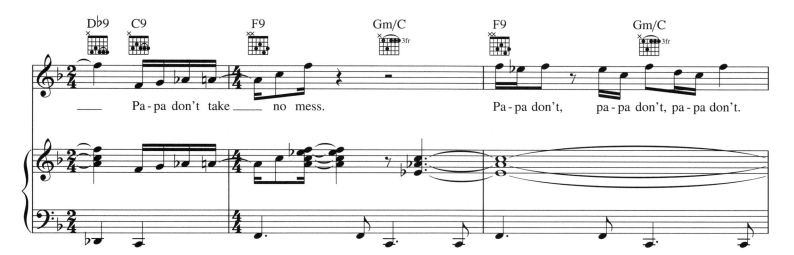

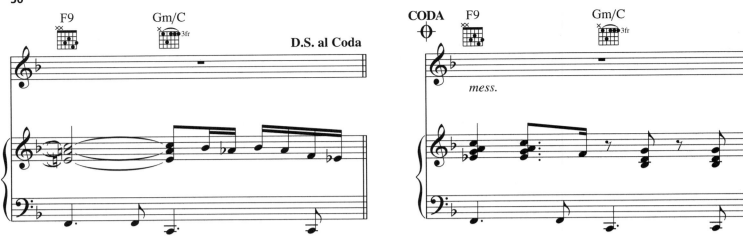

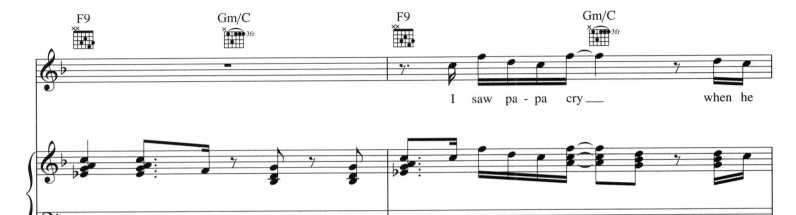

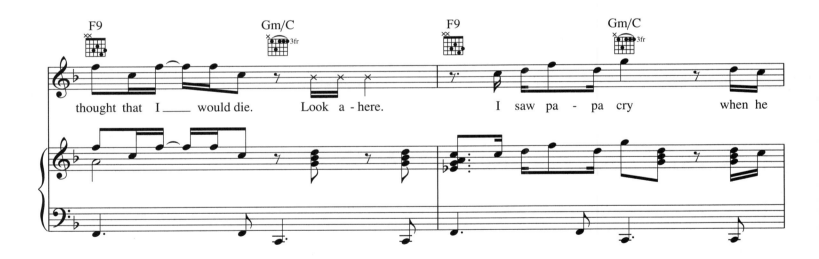

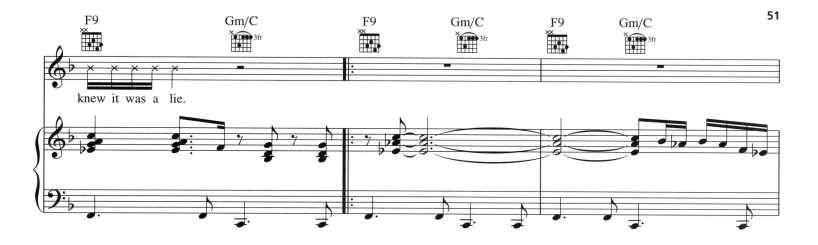

knew it was a lie.

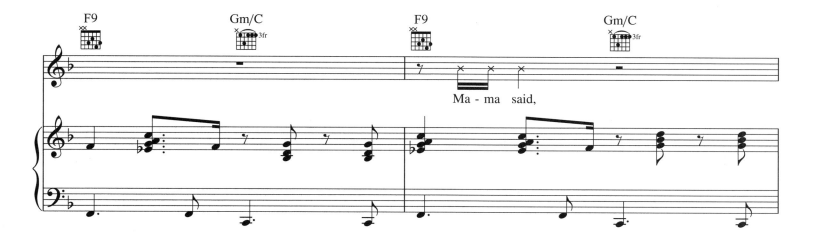

Ma - ma said,

"Pa - pa's smart. ___ Pa - pa got a whole lot - ta heart." And

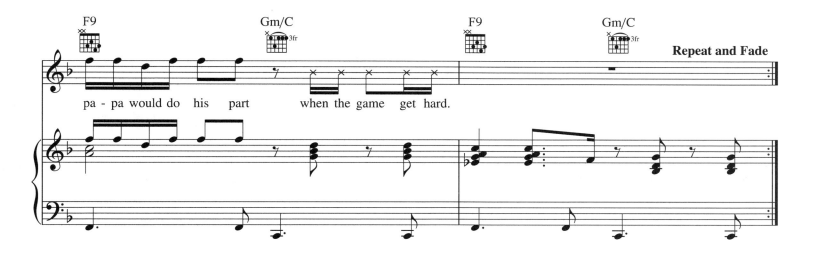

Repeat and Fade

pa - pa would do his part when the game get hard.

LIVING IN AMERICA

from the Motion Picture ROCKY IV

Words and Music by DAN HARTMAN
and CHARLIE MIDNIGHT

Medium Funk

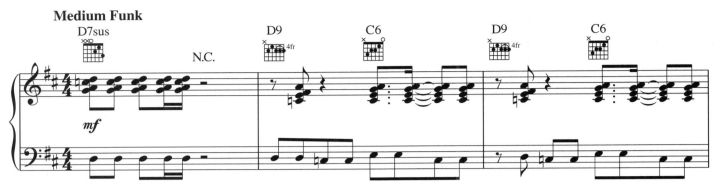

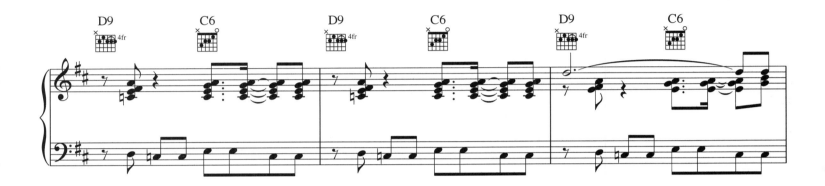

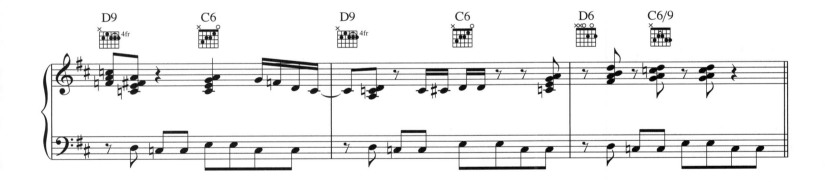

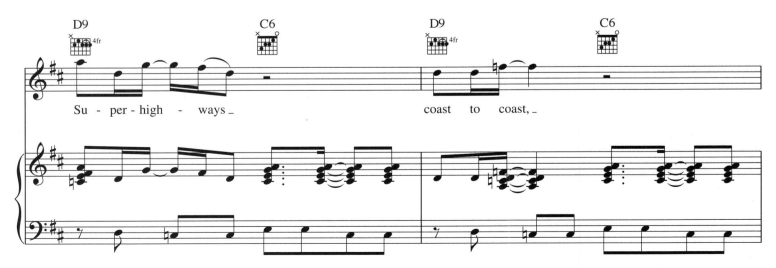

Su-per-high-ways _ coast to coast, _

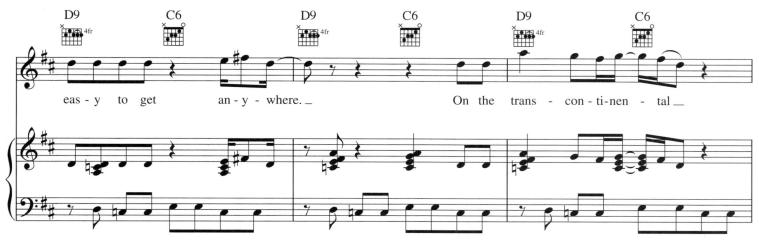

eas-y to get an-y-where. _ On the trans-con-ti-nen-tal _

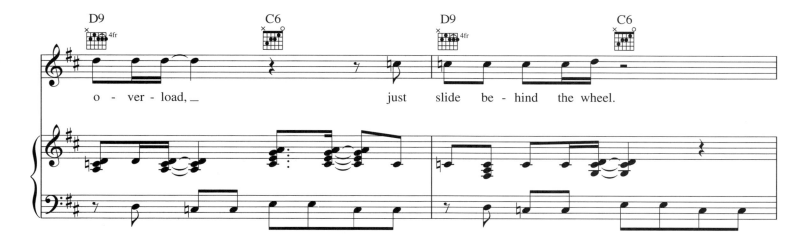

o-ver-load, _ just slide be-hind the wheel.

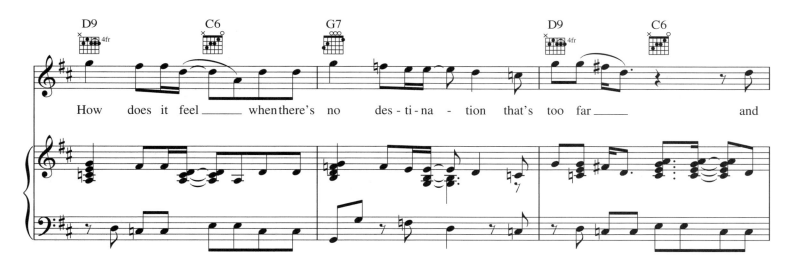

How does it feel _ when there's no des-ti-na-tion that's too far _ and

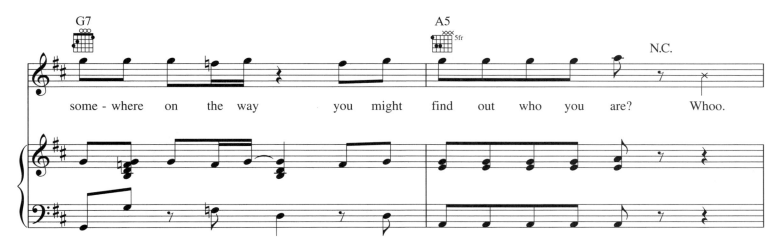

some-where on the way you might find out who you are? Whoo.

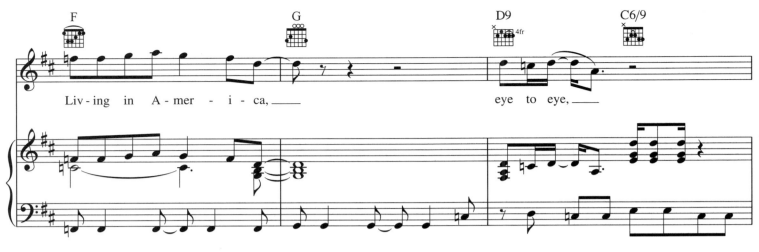

Liv-ing in A-mer-i-ca, _____ eye to eye, _____

sta-tion to sta-tion. Liv-ing in A-mer-i-ca,

hand to hand, _____ a-cross the na-tion. Liv-ing in A-mer-i-ca.

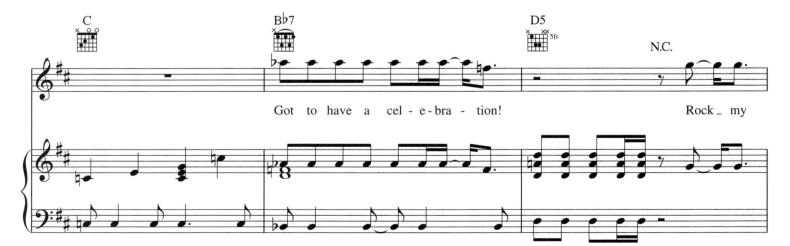

Got to have a cel-e-bra-tion! Rock _ my

ev-'ry-bod-y's work-in' o - ver-time. Liv-ing in A-mer - i - ca,
Instrumental solo

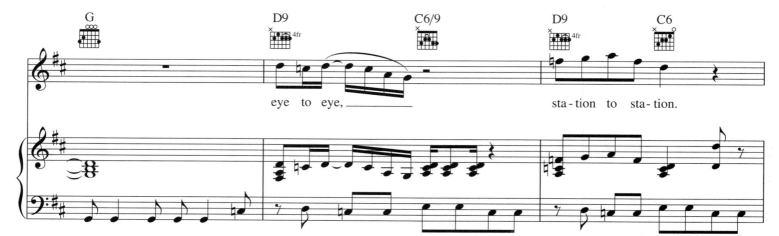

eye to eye, sta-tion to sta-tion.

Liv-ing in A-mer - i - ca, hand to hand,

'cross the na - tion. Liv-ing in A-mer - i - ca.

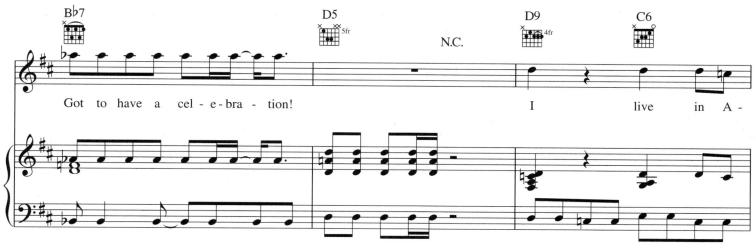

Got to have a cel-e-bra-tion! I live in A-

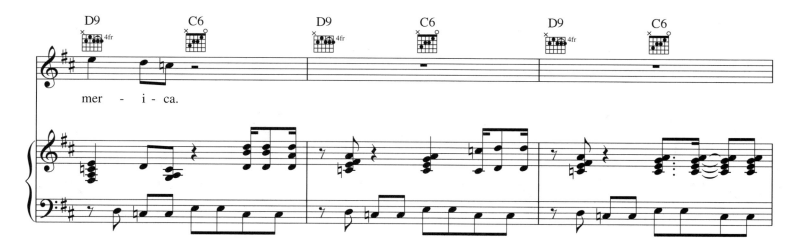

mer - i - ca.

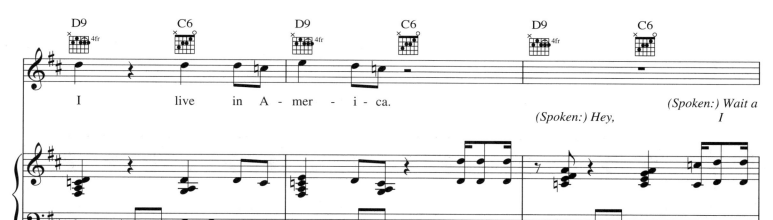

I live in A-mer-i-ca.

(Spoken:) Hey, (Spoken:) Wait a I

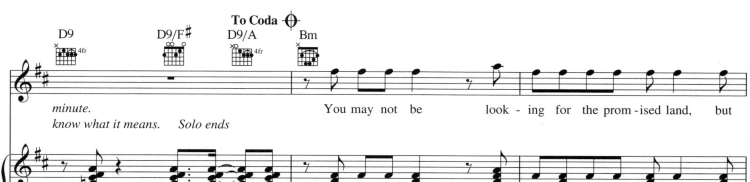

minute. You may not be look-ing for the prom-ised land, but

know what it means. Solo ends

CODA

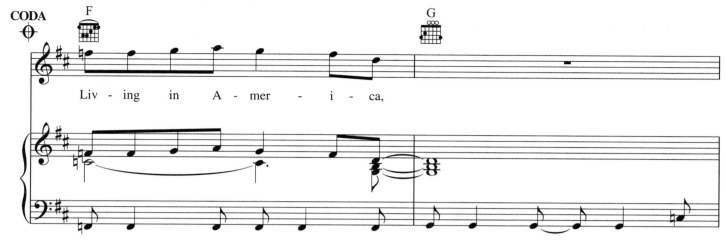

Liv - ing in A - mer - i - ca,

eye to eye, ____ sta - tion to sta - tion. Liv - ing in A - mer - i - ca,

so nice ____ with your bad self.

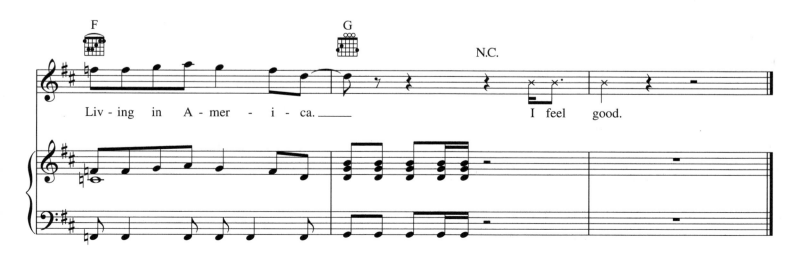

Liv - ing in A - mer - i - ca. ____ I feel good.

LOST SOMEONE

Words and Music by JAMES BROWN,
LLOYD STALLWORTH and BOBBY BYRD

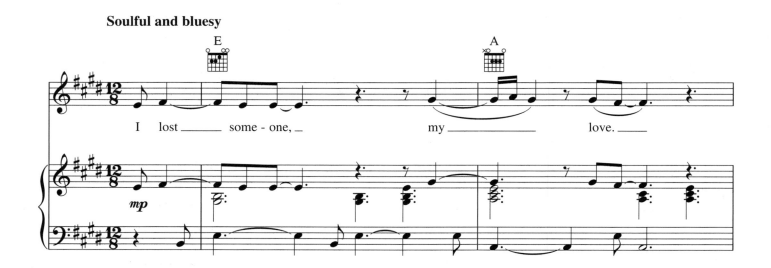

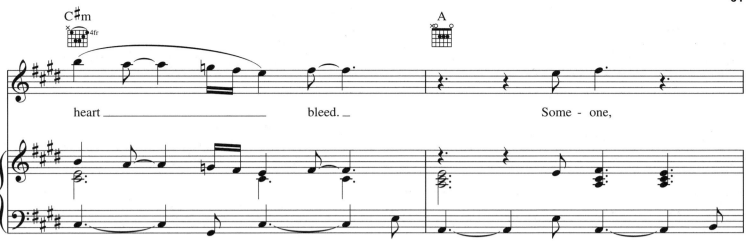

heart _____ bleed. __ Some - one,

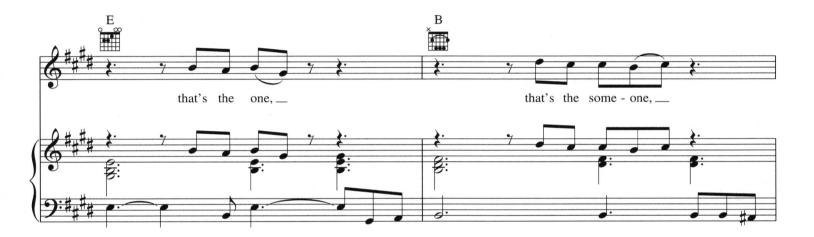

that's the one, __ that's the some - one, __

that's the some - one _____ that I _____ lost.

Don't go to stran - gers, _____

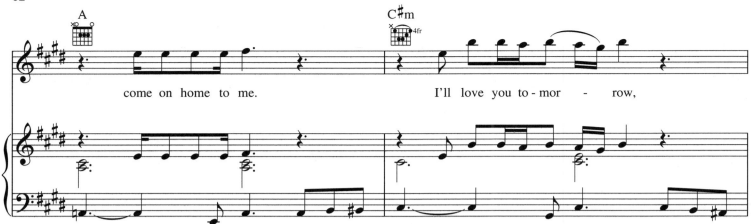

come on home to me.   I'll love you to-mor - row,

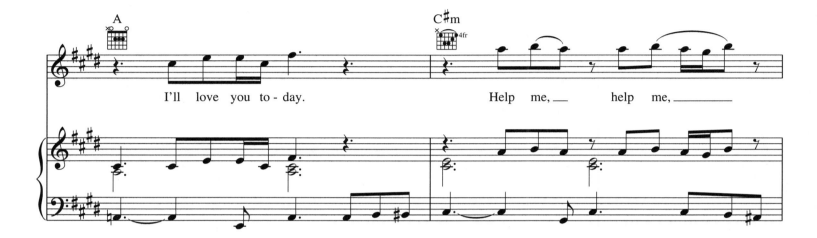

I'll love you to-day.   Help me, ___ help me, _____

I'm so weak.   Gee whiz, I love _____ you,   I'm so

weak. _   I'll love _ you to-mor - row.

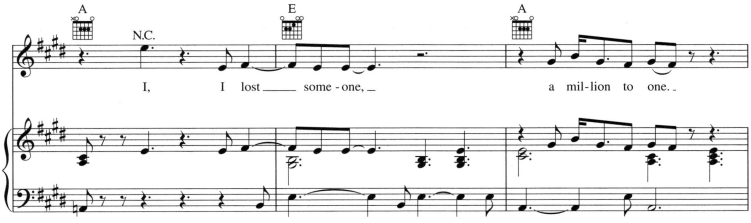

I, I lost ___ some-one, ___ a mil-lion to one. ___

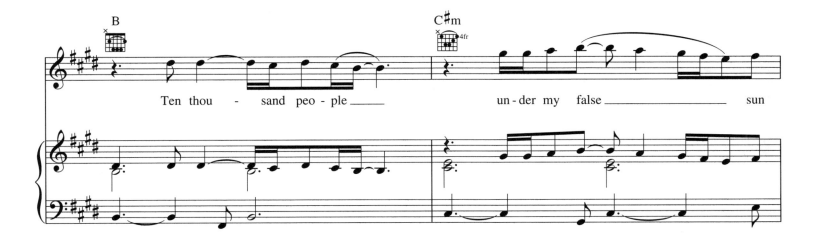

Ten thou - sand peo - ple ___ un-der my false ___ sun

who need some-one. Some-one, ___ the on - ly one,

that some - one who needs some - one un-der ___

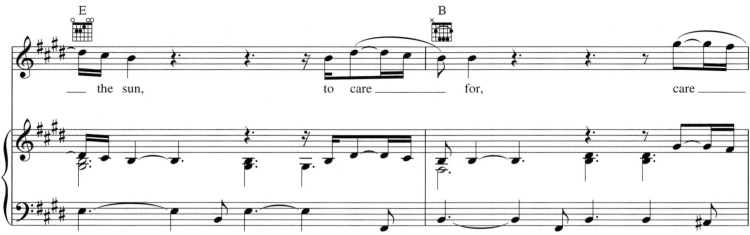

the sun, to care _____ for, care _____

_____ for, just that _____ some - one. _____

I'll love _____ you to-mor - row

like I love you to-day. I'm so _____ weak, _____ a - don't,

a - don't take my heart ___ a - way. ___ Come on, _____ come on. _____

___ A - gee whiz, I love ___ you, and don't go to stran -

- gers. Come on home _ to me, _____ come on home _ to me. ___

Repeat and Fade

___ Come on home _ to me, _ ___

Optional Ending

MAKE IT FUNKY, PT. 1

Words and Music by JAMES BROWN
and CHARLES BOBBITT

Slow Funk

Make it funk-y! Make it funk-y! Make it

funk-y! I got-ta make it funk-y! Make it funk-y! (Make it

funk-y!) Tell me, (Make it funk-y!) So it is. (Make it funk-y!) Got to do it, now. (Make it

funk-y!) Got to do it, now. (Make it funk-y!) Got to do it, now. (Make it funk-y!) Oh, yes. (Make it

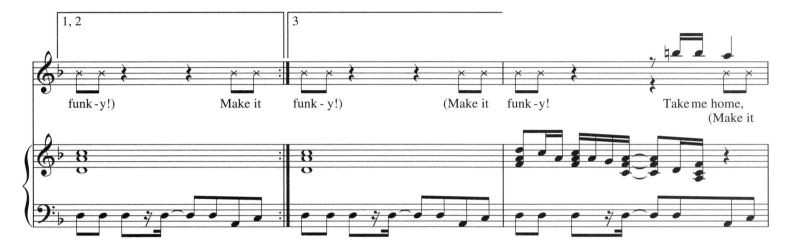

1, 2

funk-y!) Make it funk-y!)

3

(Make it funk-y! Take me home, (Make it

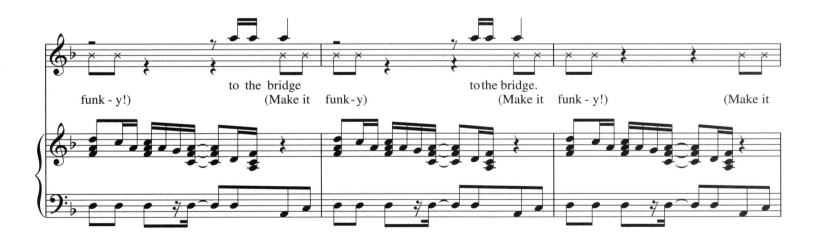

to the bridge to the bridge.

funk - y!) (Make it funk-y) (Make it funk-y!) (Make it

G9

Repeat and Fade

funk - y!)

MOTHER POPCORN, PT. 1

Words and Music by JAMES BROWN
and ALFRED JAMES ELLIS

I like 'em proud. And when they walk, you

know they draw _ a crowd. See,

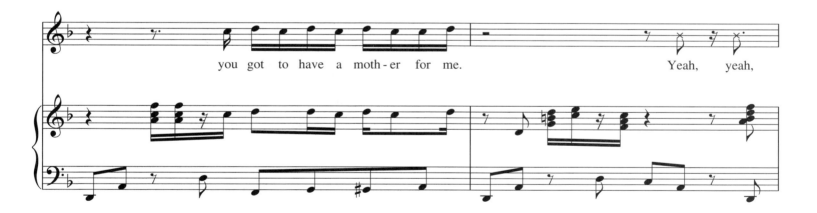

you got to have a moth-er for me. Yeah, yeah,

yeah, _____ pop-corn. Look here.

And when I___ get burnt, I use a salve.
When you do your lit - tle thing, step in a small ring.

To Coda ⊕

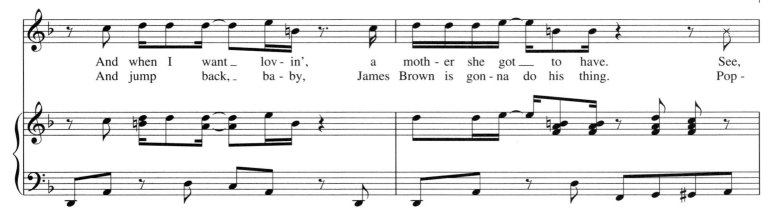

And when I want___ lov - in', a moth - er she got___ to have. See,
And jump back,___ ba - by, James Brown is gon - na do his thing. Pop -

to have a moth - er for me.

Yeah, pop - corn. Aah, ___ uh.

Yeah, ___ yeah, yeah, yeah. ___

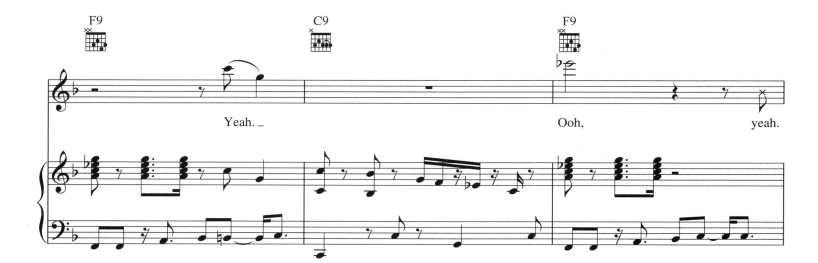

Yeah. ___ Ooh, yeah.

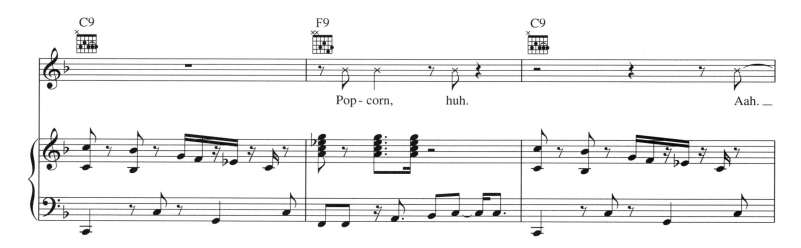

Pop - corn, huh. Aah. ___

Aah, ___ pop - corn.

Play 4 times

Vocal ad lib.

D.S. al Coda

CODA

corn.

Yeah __ yeah, yeah. _____

Optional Ending

Repeat and Fade

Vocal ad lib. to end

MY THANG

Words and Music by
JAMES BROWN

good.
me,
(What you say.)
gim-me my thing.
Let's get it on.
(What you say.)
Gim-
Gim-

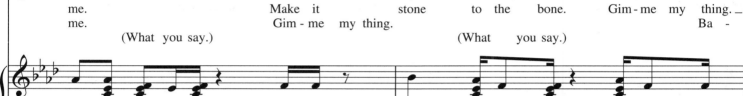

me.
me.
(What you say.)
Make it stone to the bone.
Gim-me my thing.
Gim-me my thing.
(What you say.)
Ba-

by,
(What you say.)
just gim-me some more.
Gim-me,
gim-me my thing.
(What you say.)

Fm7   Bb/F   Fm7   Bb/F

Squeeze me,
(What you say.)
Ba-by,
hold me,

got just   what I want.   Ow! _
roll me.   Ow!

___ ___   ___ ___   ow! ___
Make me,   make me scream.   Feels so good,   Make me feel.

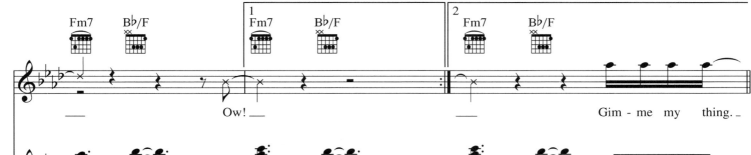

Ow! ___   Gim - me my thing. _

Play 9 times

___ *Section 1: (See additional lyrics)*

Gim - me, oh yeah. _____ babe. _____

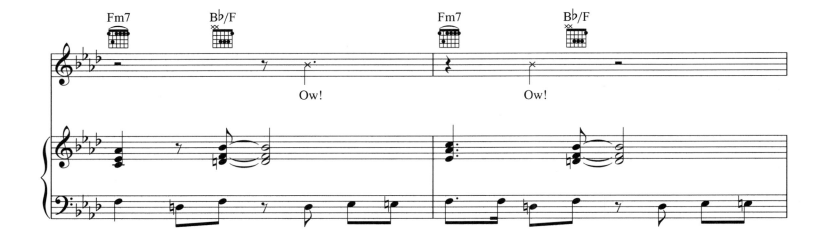

Ow! Ow!

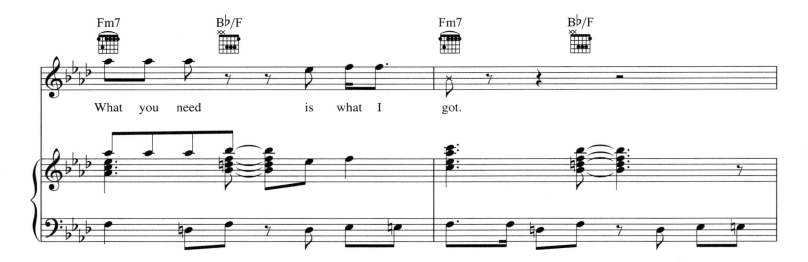

What you need is what I got.

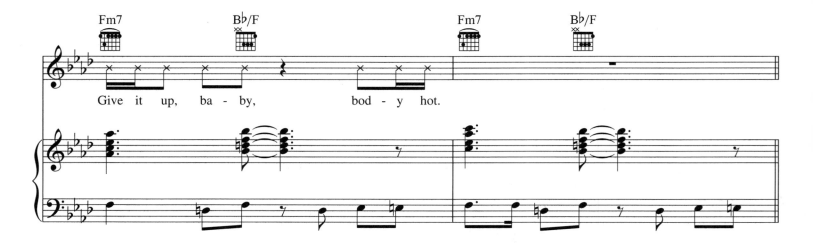

Give it up, ba - by, bod - y hot.

Section 2: (See additional lyrics)

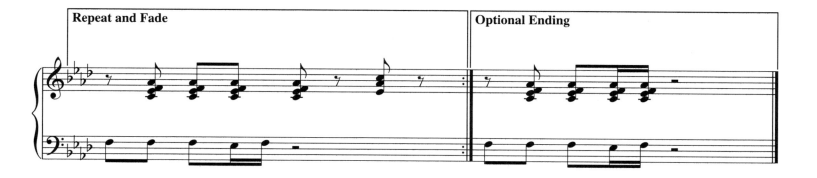

Additional Lyrics

Section 1: Gimme. I need you, baby.
I need you now.
I don't care what momma don't like.
Give it to me anyhow.
Gimme, gimme my thing.
What you got, what I need.
What you need, what I got.
Make me feel, body hot.
Gimme, gimme my thing.
Takin' off my shirt,
'Bout to work me to death.
Gimme, gimme my thing.
Gimme, ooh, ooh, ooh.
Ah, baby, baby.
Gimme, gimme my thing.
Gimme, gimme, gimme, gimme.

Section 2: I wanna be satisfied.
Oh, you can't get it
Keepin' it all inside.
Now gimme, gimme my thing.
Oh, give, I said gimme my thing.
Oh God, gimme my thing.
Help me cross, help me cross.
If you don't help me,
I'll do it myself.
Gimme, gimme my thing.

PAPA'S GOT A BRAND NEW BAG

Words and Music by
JAMES BROWN

Moderate Funk

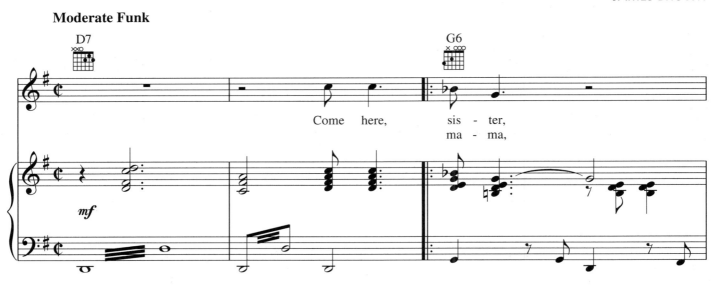

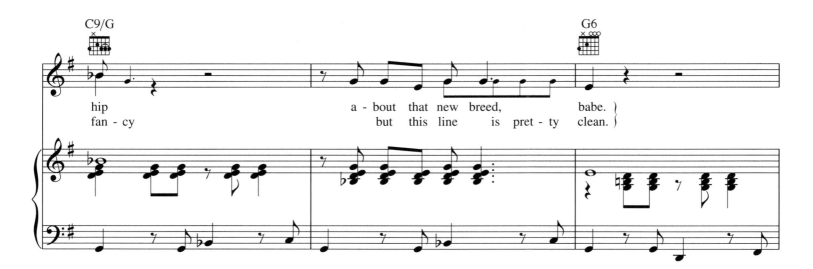

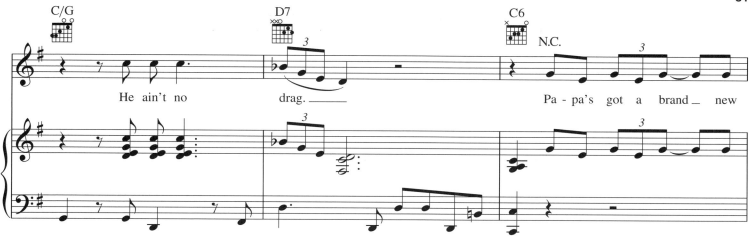

He ain't no drag. _____ Pa-pa's got a brand _ new

bag. _____ *1.* Come here, *2.* He's do-ing the

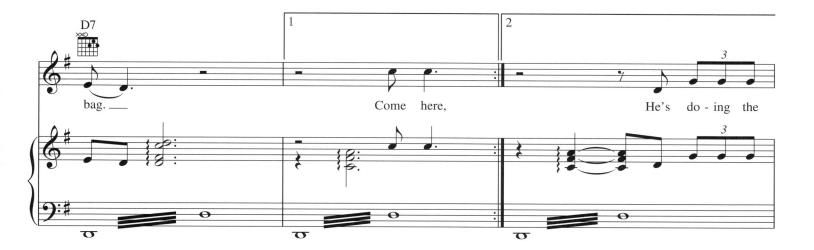

Jerk. He's do-ing the Fly. Don't play him cheap 'cause you know he ain't

shy. He's do-ing the Mon-key, the Mashed Po -

ta - toes. Jump back, Jack, see you lat - er, al - li - ga - tor. Come here,

sis - ter, Pa - pa's in the swing.

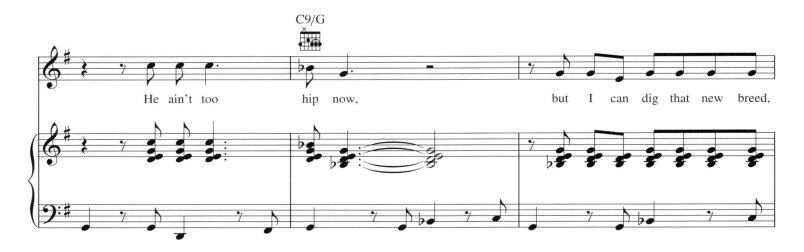

He ain't too hip now, but I can dig that new breed,

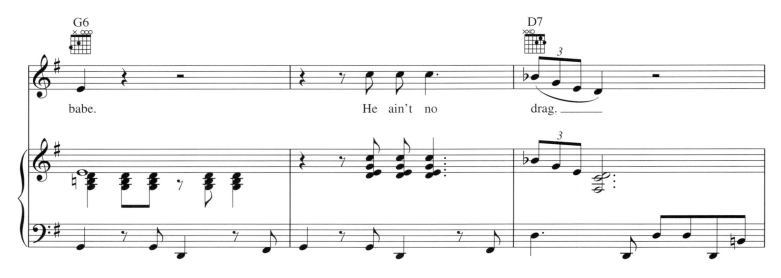

babe. He ain't no drag. _____

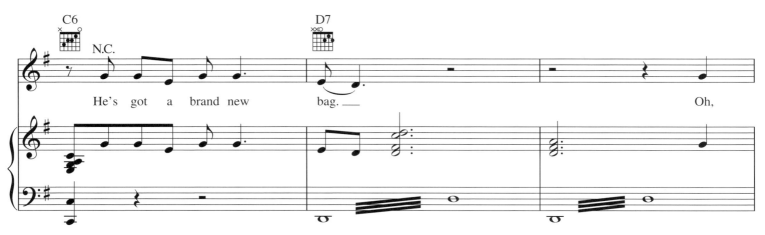

He's got a brand new bag. ___ Oh,

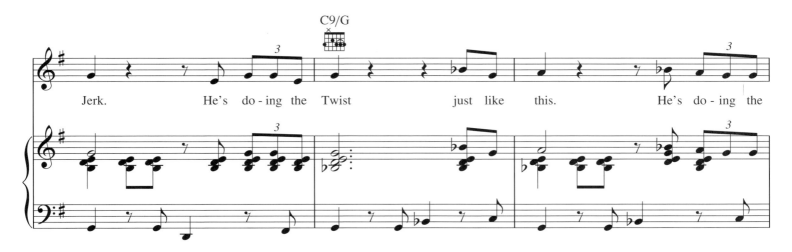

Pa - pa, he's do - ing the Jerk. Pa - pa, he's do - ing the

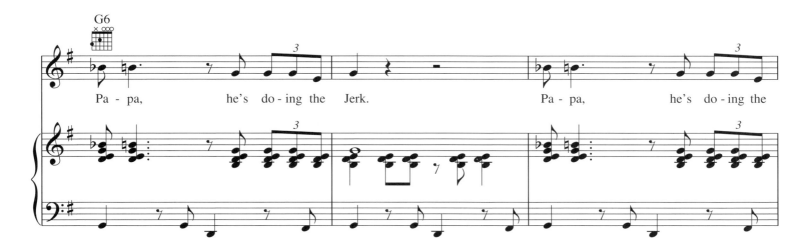

Jerk. He's do - ing the Twist just like this. He's do - ing the

Fly ev - 'ry day and ev - 'ry night. The thing's ___

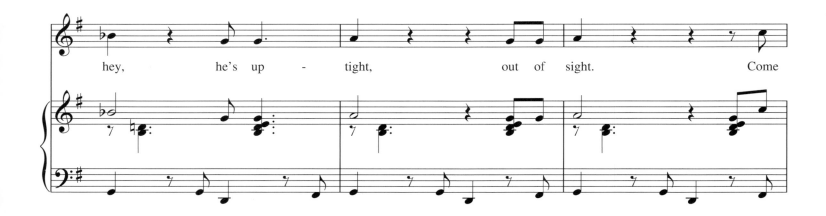

THE PAYBACK

Words and Music by JAMES BROWN,
FRED WESLEY and JOHN STARKS

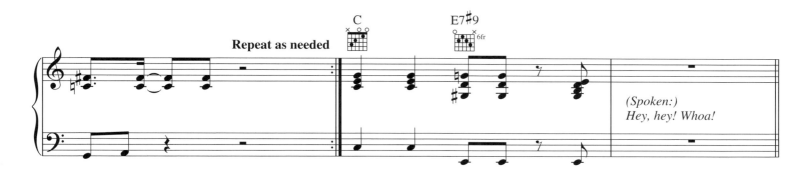

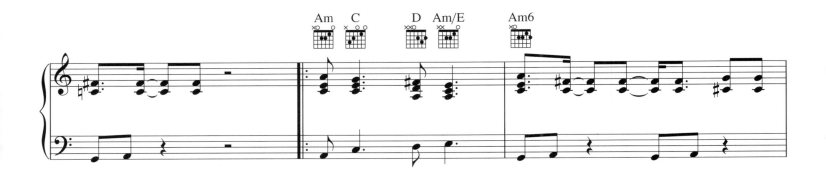

Verses

1. You get down with my girfriend; that ain't right.
   You holler and cuss; you wanna fight.
   Payback is the thing you got to see.
   Hell, you never do any damn thing to me.

   You sold me out for check and change.
   You told me today they had it all arranged.
   They had me down, and that's a fact.
   And now you're pumped.
   You gotta get ready for the big payback (the big payback).
   That's where I land for the big payback (the big payback).

   I can do wheelin', I can do dealin' (yes you can)
   But I don't do no damn squealin'.
   I can dig rappin', I'm ready. I can dig scrappin'.
   But I can't dig that back-stabbin' (oh no).
   Now, brother, get ready, that's a fact.
   Get ready, you mother, for the big payback.
   Let me hit 'em, hit 'em, Fred, hit 'em.

2. You took my money, you got my honey.
   Don't want me to see what you're doin' to me.
   I can get back; I gotta deal with you.
   Gotta deal with ya; gotta deal with ya.
   I gotta deal with ya. Let me tell ya,

   You get down with my woman; that ain't right.
   You holler and cuss; you wanna fight.
   Don't do me no darn favor.
   I don't know karate but I know crazy (yes we do).
   Get ready, that's a fact.
   Get ready, you mother, for the big payback (the big payback).

   I'm a man, I'm a man, I'm the son of a man.
   If I don't take care of you, then Papa can.
   Get ready for the big payback (the big payback).
   Hit me again.

3. Lord, Lord, get ready.
   I need it. I need a hit again.
   The same one, the same one, the same one.
   Hear the band.

4. You sold me out for check and change.
   You said my woman had it all arranged.
   She tried to make a deal; she wanted to squeal
   But I had my boys on her heals.

   I saw her when she come in town' the line.
   She broke down when she wanted to cry.
   I don't care what she does; she's gonna be doin' just like she was.

   Take those kids and raise 'em up.
   Show 'em how to drink up the righteous cup.
   Take her, take that woman. There's one place she's bound.
   Just run that mother outa town.
   Make her get up; make her get up, get out.
   Make her get up; make her get up, get out.
   I'm mad; I want revenge; I want revenge.
   My patience ends on revenge; my patience ends on revenge.
   I want revenge; I want revenge (the big payback)
   Can I get some hits? I need those hits; I need those hits.
   Hit me.
   Lord, I need those hits, carry on.
   The big payback.

PLEASE, PLEASE, PLEASE

Words and Music by JAMES BROWN
and JOHNNY TERRY

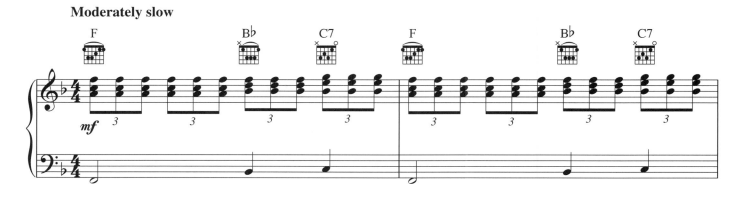

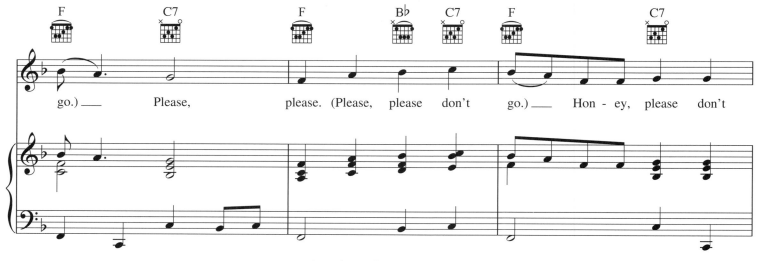

1. Please, please, please, please. (Please, please don't
2., 3. see additional lyrics

go.) ___ Please, please. (Please, please don't go.) ___ Hon-ey, please don't

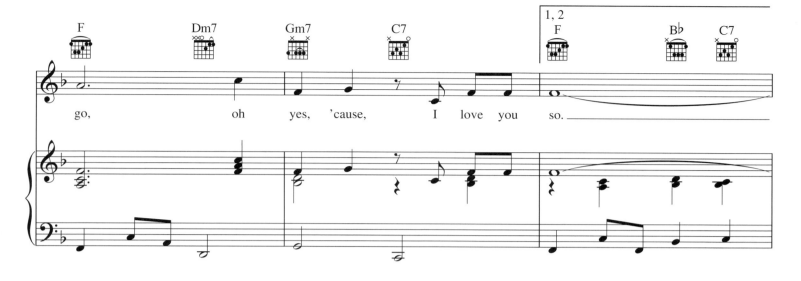

go,   oh   yes,   'cause,   I   love   you   so. _____

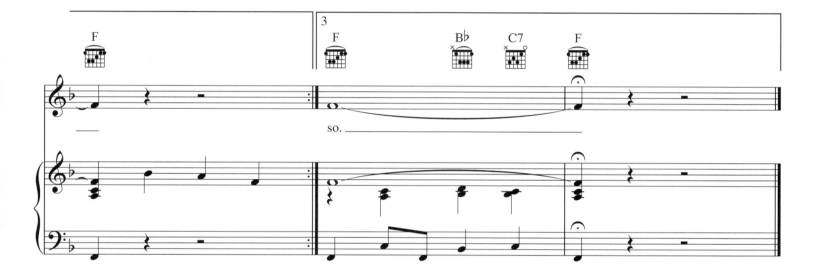

so. _____

Additional Lyrics

1. Baby, you've done me wrong. (You've done me wrong.)
   Baby, you've done me wrong. (You've done me wrong.)
   Baby, you've done me wrong. (You've done me wrong.)
   Took my love and now you're gone.

2. Baby, take my hand. (Please take my hand)
   I want to be your lover man. (Please take my hand)
   Honey, please don't go. I love you so.

SAY IT LOUD
(I'm Black and I'm Proud)

Words and Music by JAMES BROWN
and ALFRED JAMES ELLIS

D.S. and Fade
(with repeats)

Spoken Lyrics

1. Say it loud: "I'm black and I'm proud."
   Say it loud: "I'm black and I'm proud."
   Some people say we got a lot of malice,
   Some say it's a lot of nerve
   But I say we won't quit moving until we get what we deserve.
   We've been 'buked and we've been scorned,
   We've been treated bad, talked about as sure as you're born.
   But just as sure as it takes two eyes to make a pair.
   Brother we can't quit until we get our share.
   Say it loud: "I'm black and I'm proud."
   Say it loud: "I'm black and I'm proud."
   Say it loud: "I'm black and I'm proud."
   I've worked on jobs with my feet and my hands,
   But all that work I did was for the other man.
   Now we demand a chance to do things for ourselves.
   We're tired of beating our head against the wall
   And working for someone else.
   Say it loud: "I'm black and I'm proud." (4 times)

Bridge: Ooh-ee, you're killing me.
   Alright, you're outa sight,
   Alright, so tough, you're tough enough.
   Ooh-ee, you're killing me.

2. Say it loud: "I'm black and I'm proud."
   Say it loud: "I'm black and I'm proud."
   Now we demand a chance to do things for ourselves.
   We're tired of beating our heads against the wall
   And working for someone else.
   We're people, we're like the birds and the bees,
   But we'd rather die on our feet than keep living on our knees.
   Say it loud: "I'm black and I'm proud." (3 times)

Fade on Bridge

SOUL POWER

Words and Music by
JAMES BROWN

to me. (Soul power.) Hey! We need _ it. (Soul power.) We want _

_ it. (Soul power.) Got to have it. (Soul power.) I

wan - na get un - der your skin.

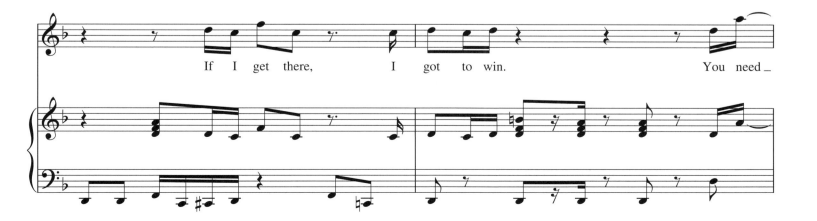

If I get there, I got to win. You need _

some soul. Come on, __ get some and

then you'll know where I'm com-in' from. __ Huh,

I may lay in the cut and go a-long, __ but

I'm still on the case, __ and my rap is strong, __ uh.

Hey!   Don't jump _

_ on my train   when I'm out of sight.   Just

check your-self,   and say,   yeah, you're right.   Huh.

G9

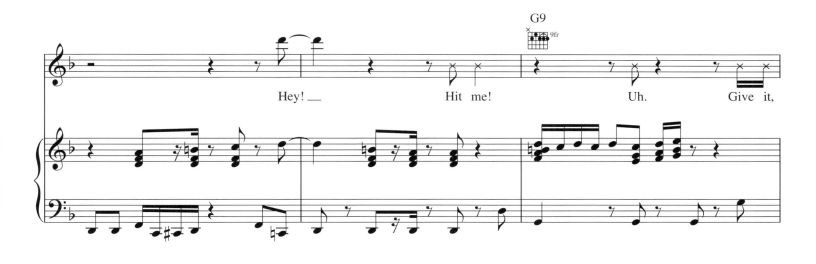

Hey! _   Hit me!   Uh.   Give it,

-der, ah, ___ love me slow. That don't

To Coda ⊕

get it, come back for more. Hey! ___

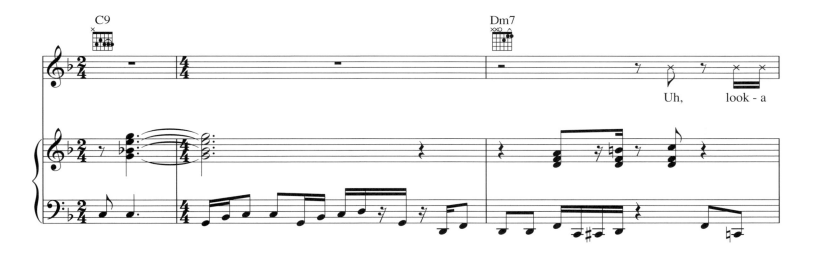

C9 Dm7

Uh, look-a

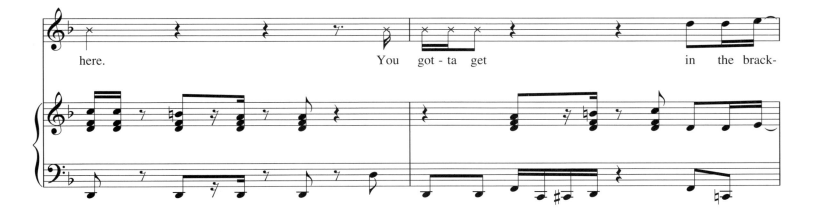

here. You got-ta get in the brack-

-et. You know I like ___ it. Huh, al - right.

Look - a here, al - right - uh.

Don't fall ___ on the ground, you got ___ to get

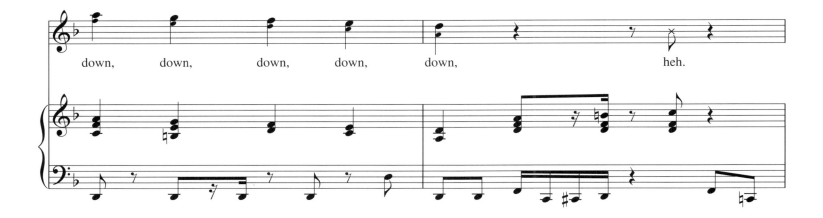

down, down, down, down, down, heh.

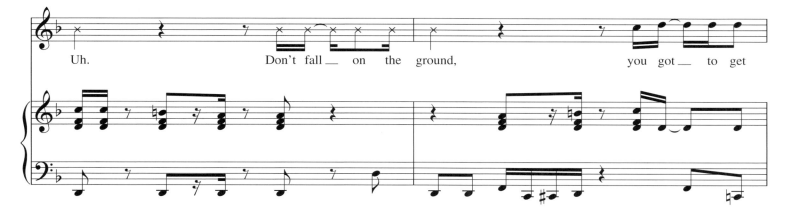

Uh. Don't fall __ on the ground, you got __ to get

down, down, down, down, down, huh, huh.

Good god. I got to ask you what we need. __

__ (Soul power.) what we want - uh. (Soul power.) Got to have,

D.S. al Coda

CODA

Help me, we got-ta, we got-ta, get in the

brack-et. Know I like it. Hey! Hey!

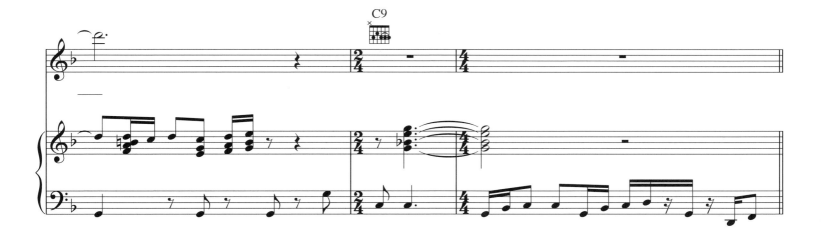

C9

Dm7

| **Repeat and Fade** | **Optional Ending** |

Instrumental solo and vocal ad libs to end

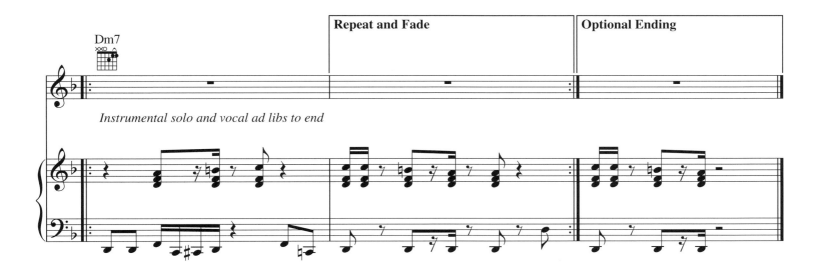

SUPER BAD SUPER SLICK

Words and Music by
JAMES BROWN

Funky Soul groove

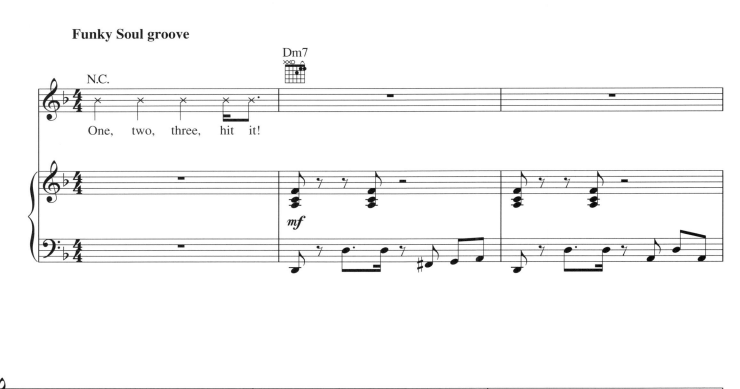

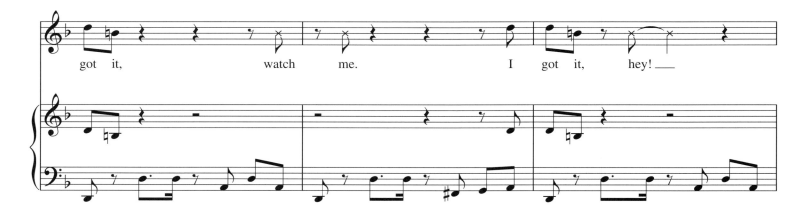

I got some-thin' that makes me wan-na shout - uh. I got some-thin' that

tells me what it's all ___ a - bout. Huh, I got soul, ___ and I'm su-per bad. _

1st time only

Dm9

I got soul, ___

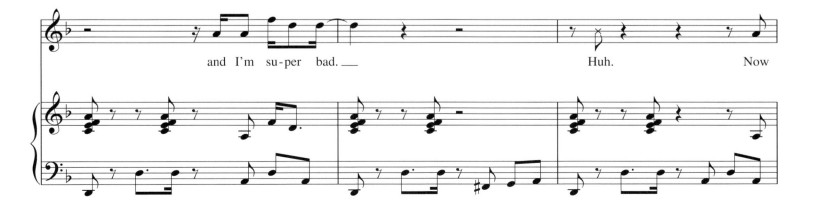

and I'm su-per bad. _ Huh. Now

peo- ple, huh, let it all hang out.

If you don't, broth-ers and sis- ters, then

To Coda ⊕

you won't know, huh, what it's all a- bout.

Gim - me, gim- me, gim- me,

gim - me,   gim - me,   gim -

me,   gim - me,   hey! ___

A7#9   D9   **Play 3 times**

Whee!   *Instrumental solo and vocal ad lib.*

D.S. al Coda

Gim- me, gim- me, gim-

me, gim - me, hey! _

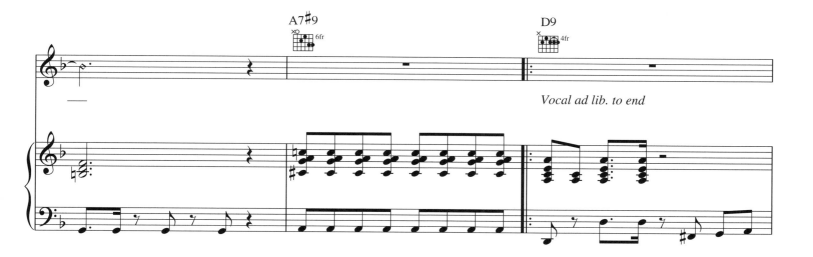

A7#9   D9

_

Vocal ad lib. to end

Optional Ending

Repeat and Fade

TRY ME

Words and Music by
JAMES BROWN

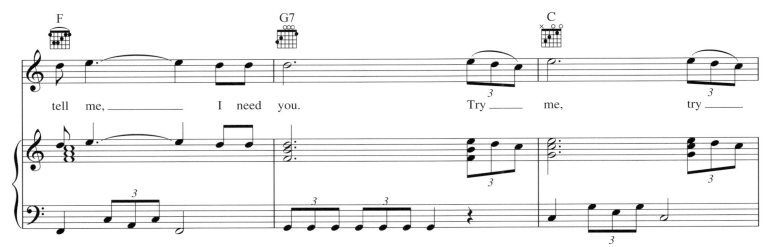

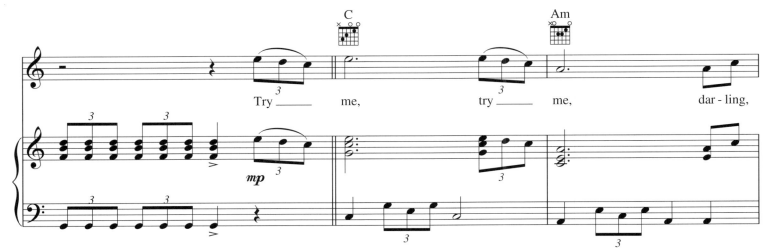